To dear Emma   Christmas 1984
All our Love
        Mummy & Daddy x x x x

In the Beginning

CREATION MYTHS FROM AROUND THE WORLD

Concept and illustrations by

HELEN CHERRY

Stories retold by

KENNETH McLEISH

LONGMAN

Acknowledgements

The following anthropologists and mythologists are gratefully acknowledged by Helen Cherry for their work which provided source material.
Ulli Beier *The origin of life and death* (African creation myths), Heinemann 1966; G Buhler trans. *The laws of Manu*; C H Goeje *Philosophy initiation and myths of Guiana and adjacent countries*, International Archiv für Ethnographie, Supplement 44, 1943; R Graves ed. *The Larousse encyclopaedia of mythology*, Hamlyn 1969; George Grey *Polynesian mythology*, Whitticombe and Tombs 1956; S N Kramer ed. *Mythologies of the ancient world*, Doubleday 1961; C P Mountford *The Tiwi*, Phoenix 1958; I Nicholson *Mexican and Central American mythology*, Hamlyn 1967; Alfonso Ortiz *The Tewa world*, University of Chicago Press 1969; James Teit *The Jessup North Pacific expedition* 1913.

LONGMAN GROUP LIMITED
Longman House, Burnt Mill, Harlow, Essex CM20 2JE, England, and Associated Companies throughout the World

First published 1984
ISBN 0 582 25083 8

Set in 14/15 Sabon Monophoto
Printed in Great Britain by Blantyre Printing & Binding Co Limited

Contents

In the Beginning

How did the universe begin? Who decided on the planets, the sun and moon, the stars, the earth? How were our seas and continents made – and why? Who created the millions of plants, insects, birds, fish and animals that live on earth?

Since the human race itself began, we have tried to find answers to questions such as these. Modern scientists say that the universe resulted from enormous explosions in space, or from a process as gradual and purposeful as water wearing away a stone; they say that life on earth began with a chance chemical reaction at the one moment when conditions were exactly right, and that from that single accident all plants and animals (including ourselves) evolved. But as well as scientific explanations, there are others: stories made up and handed down for thousands of years, growing ever more detailed and fanciful on the way.

Creation-stories were told in every human settlement on earth, from the deserts of Australia to the grass-plains of America, from lush tropical islands to the glaciers and volcanoes of Iceland. Each of the fourteen stories in this book is a different account of the same events, suited to the climate and lifestyle of the people who first told it. Some (*Ra, Fire-lords, The Dance of Life*) were part of ancient religions which no one now believes in; others (*Under-earth, Over-earth, Amana and her Children, Old-spider and her Helpers*) stayed in one small place, and were known only to a single tribe or people; two (*Seven Days* and *Brahma and Sarasvati*) come from important modern world religions, whose followers consider them not tales at all, but true.

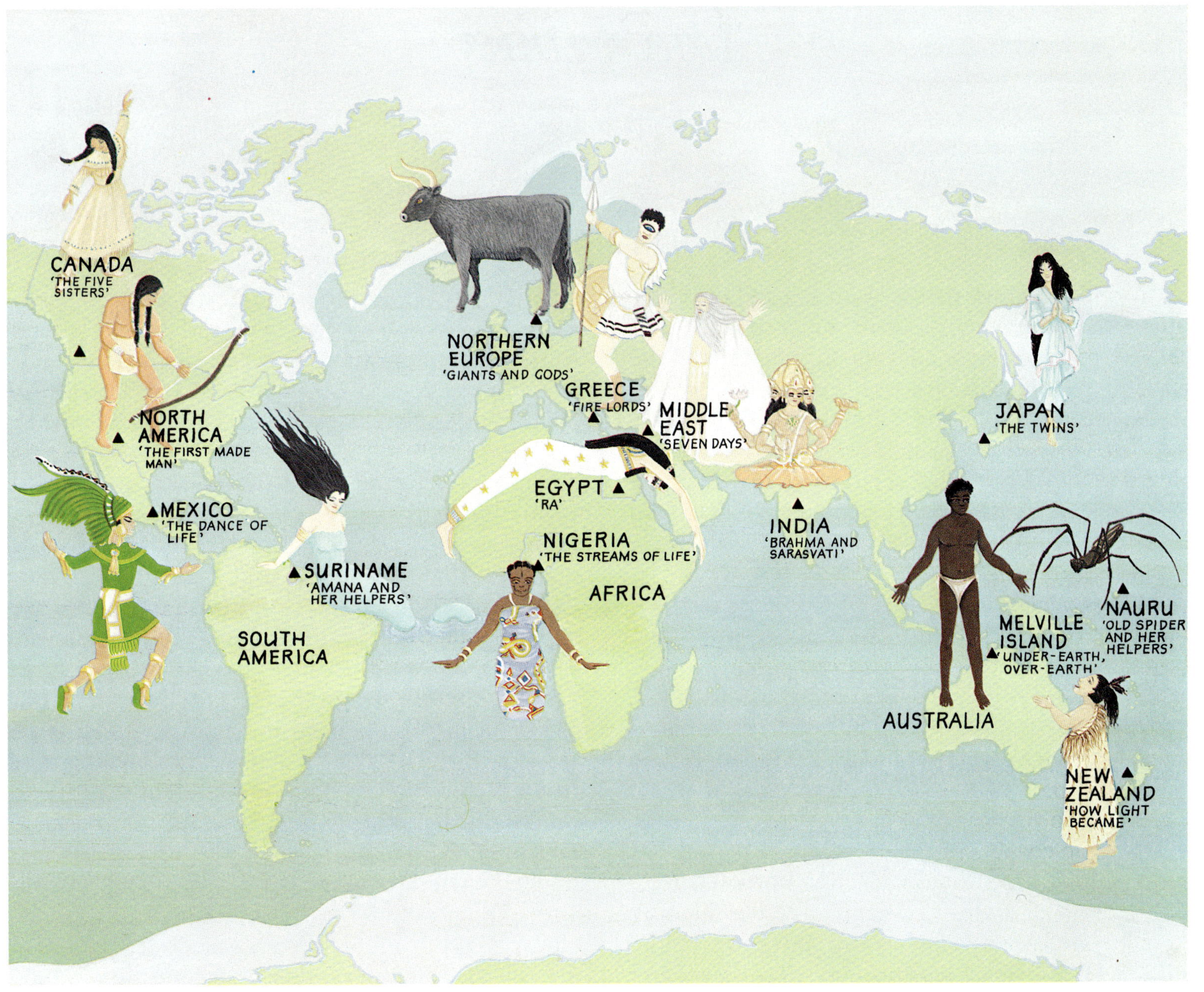

CANADA
'THE FIVE SISTERS'
NORTH AMERICA
'THE FIRST MADE MAN'
MEXICO
'THE DANCE OF LIFE'
SURINAME
'AMANA AND HER HELPERS'
SOUTH AMERICA
NORTHERN EUROPE
'GIANTS AND GODS'
GREECE
'FIRE LORDS'
EGYPT
'RA'
NIGERIA
'THE STREAMS OF LIFE'
AFRICA
MIDDLE EAST
'SEVEN DAYS'
INDIA
'BRAHMA AND SARASVATI'
JAPAN
'THE TWINS'
AUSTRALIA
MELVILLE ISLAND
'UNDER-EARTH, OVER-EARTH'
NAURU
'OLD SPIDER AND HER HELPERS'
NEW ZEALAND
'HOW LIGHT BECAME'

The Twins

At first, everything in the universe bubbled like soup in a pot; at the bottom, mud steamed and heaved, bubbling up from time to time to stain the sea above. One day fire, ice, continents, winds, rocks, trees, people and animals would emerge, but for now their elements slopped together, blending and separating, separating and blending in ceaseless, restless movement. High overhead was the chilly gulf of space; in between billowed a cloud-bridge, grey as ice.

As the elements of creation swirled and seethed, a seed settled in the mud, burst apart, put down roots and began to grow. A green shoot fingered its way from the swamp below to the gulf above, reaching out for the light of distant stars. As it grew it branched and split, and with each new splitting a pair of twin gods, brother and sister, was born. Soon there were seven pairs, one in each of the seven corners of the universe.

For a long time no new life was born. Then an eighth pair of twins, Isanami and her brother Isanagi, appeared. They stood shivering in the cold, high air. They had no idea who they were, where to go or what to do. Then, in a single angry rush, their fourteen brothers and sisters surged round them from the corners of the universe and began hissing, "Go down! Go down! There's no place for you here. Go down, where there's work for you to do!"

They gave Isanami and Isanagi a long-handled spear. Its shaft was made of twisted wood decorated with a sky-blue tassel; its blade was diamond-sharp. Isanami and Isanagi carried it down and stood on the cloud-bridge between the air above and the swamp below. They dipped the spear into the mud-ocean, and began stirring it. At first the mixture stayed shapeless and slippery, but gradually as they stirred it began to curdle, the way milk curdles in a churn. Its liquid parts frothed like waves; its solid parts peaked like mountains; the thickest parts of all formed clots which stuck to the spear-blade and slowed it down. When the stirring was finished and Isanami and Isanagi pulled the spear-blade clear, a mud-clot splashed from blade to sea and settled to form an island. This was the first land, the home

Isanami's and Isanagi's brothers and sisters had planned for them.

The young gods stepped down from the cloud-bridge to the island. They trod carefully, balancing against one another. Then, when they found firm ground underfoot, they began jumping, dancing and laughing, and ran eagerly across the island from end to end, exploring. They planted the spear in the centre like a pillar, and built a palace.

For years Isanami and Isanagi were utterly happy with their island. But when they had revisited each corner a hundred times, and played a thousand games of hide-and-seek through every fold and valley, they began to grow more and more tired of it. One day, at the same instant and in the same breath, they said, "Why don't we make more islands, sisters and brothers to this one?"

They ran to the place where they had long ago planted their stirring-spear. But it was now a solid pillar, far too thick to lift. "What shall we do?" said Isanagi.

"Instead of stirring-magic, let's use running-magic," answered Isanami. So they crouched down beside the pillar, and when Isanagi shouted "Go!" they ran round the island in opposite directions. When they met by the pillar again, Isanami laughed at her brother's puffed, red face and said jokingly, "What a handsome man!" He at once replied, "What a pretty woman!"

That was their running-spell. Unfortunately, for it to work properly Isanagi should have spoken first, before his sister. So instead of an island they made a hideous, helpless monster, lolling on all fours in the mud in front of them. Quickly, before they could grow fond of it, they bundled it up in reeds, dumped it in a reed-boat and floated it out to sea. Then they set out to perform the running-spell again – and this time Isanagi took care to say "What a pretty woman!" before his sister had time to say "What a handsome man!"

Now that the spell was properly performed, it worked and made a second island just like the first. Isanami and Isanagi eagerly carried on creating. They produced continents, rivers, trees, grass, shrubs and plants. They made waves, winds and weather to surround the new land, and birds, insects and animals to live on it. In the end, carried away by their own magic, they used the most powerful spell of all and made fire – and its heat scorched Isanami so badly that she fell deathly sick and knew that her time on earth was done. Like a wounded animal crawling to its lair, she burrowed through the earth's crust to the Underworld. She gathered her last strength, spoke her last spell, and turned her skull and ribs to caves and her bones to rocks. Maggots feasted on her flesh, and its magic turned them to devils, scampering and prancing in every dark corner.

So the world was made, and everything in it; and monsters and devils were accidentally made as well. After his sister's death, Isanagi fathered a family of gods and goddesses in the upper world; they included the rulers of sun, moon, sky and sea.

Brahma and Sarasvati

I N D I A : H I N D U

Before the world, sky or stars were made, there was darkness. It was everywhere, and it was empty; but for all its emptiness it was neither dead nor cold. It was warm, damp and lively, endlessly rippling and eddying throughout the universe. If people had existed and been able to see it, it would have seemed like a giant creature without shape, breathing softly as it slept. And if they had been able to listen, they would have heard its ripples gradually transform themselves to sound. A word began. At first it was no more than a whisper, but it swelled and grew to a billow of sound, a gentle syllable endlessly repeating itself, folding back on itself, coiling and twisting till it filled all space. OM ... OM ... OM ...

As the word unfolded and spread, calm as a heartbeat, it turned the rippling universe into an endless, unfathomable ocean. Deep in the water bobbed a seed – and as the ocean-currents ebbed and flowed, they carried it to the surface to become a glowing, golden egg. The egg rocked on the water, and wavetips reflected its radiance to every corner of the darkness round about. As it rocked, the sacred word "Om" went on cradling it, enfolding it the way rose-petals enfold the flower-heart deep inside. The sound was in and out and round about, and inside the eggshell, as long time passed, it formed itself into Brahma, the First Father, Creator of Worlds.

When Brahma was ready to be born, he hatched like a chick from the golden egg. From half the shell he made the sky; from the other half he made the earth; he set air between them to keep them apart. The golden sky-shell twinkled in the smoke of space like a myriad stars, or like water-drops glistening in an upturned bowl. The earth-shell bobbed on the sea, until Brahma anchored it with rocks and mountain-peaks. The air between the shells sometimes took its form from the golden light above, and was clear and pure; at other times it gathered dampness from the sea below, and blanketed the earth with storms.

When the earth was ready, Brahma drew out of himself six elements: thought, hearing, sight, touch, taste and smell. He blended the elements to make living things of every kind. He sowed the earth with plants, and gave them two gifts: the sense of touch and the power to remake themselves with seeds and fruits. He stocked the land with animals and the sea with fish, and set the air whirring with birds and insects – and to each of them he gave seven gifts: the senses of touch, taste, hearing, sight, and smell, the power to reproduce themselves and the power of movement. The world throbbed with life, as its new creatures squawked, hissed, chattered, buzzed, yelped, whistled and barked on every side.

So Brahma created all living things, and gave them gifts. One thing only he kept from them: thought. The world was their playground, and they had senses to enjoy it – why should they need thought as well? Until the time came when he made a creature worthy of possessing intelligence, Brahma locked it inside himself. Many ages passed, and he spent them roaming the world, delighting in his own creation. Sometimes he rode a white swan, sometimes a peacock; sometimes he sailed across seas and rivers in a lotus-boat. With his four hands he picked up all kinds of objects and carried them: a pink lotus-flower, a string of prayer-beads, a sacred book, a golden pot.

After a time, Brahma divided himself and made another being, Sarasvati. As soon as she existed, Brahma fell passionately in love with her. He gazed fondly at her, and she lowered her eyes and modestly stepped to one side, out of his gaze. At once a second head appeared on Brahma's neck, gazing at her lovingly as before. She stepped behind him, and a third head grew; she stepped to his other side, and a fourth head grew; she soared into the air above him, and a fifth head grew, looking up. Brahma said, "Come down, Sarasvati. Help me make angels to live in light, demons to live in darkness, and the human race to live on earth." Sarasvati swooped back down to earth and married him. They spent their wedding night (of a hundred years) in a secret cave, and at the end of it Manu, the first human being, was born. Brahma gave him eight gifts: five senses, the powers of movement and reproduction, and the greatest gift of all, the power of intelligent thought.

Ever since then, the world has belonged to human beings, insects, birds and animals. The gods, and the angels and demons they created, watch over us and help or punish us as we deserve. Brahma's fifth head, the one looking up into the sky, burned away long ago in the fiery stare of Shiva, god of destruction. He soars now in the emptiness of space, rides swans or peacocks on earth as before, or sits beside Sarasvati on lotuses in quiet streams. She is the goddess of knowledge and of all the arts, especially music. She holds flowers, prayer-beads, finger-drums or a palm-leaf book; she plays a wire-stringed veena, and her music fills the world with the sweetness of the gods.

The Dance of Life

MEXICO

The God of All made air, water, earth and every creature that lives in them. For a time he held them in his hand, and they were like a sand-speck hanging in a water-drop. But soon he went about other business, and left the beings of the universe to manage their own affairs. As soon as his back was turned, Earth grew crocodile jaws, gobbled every other creature she could find, then dived into Water and hid there, snapping at everything that came her way.

Of the beings left uneaten, the bravest were Wind and Shadow. They made a plan to swim down, catch Earth off-guard and force her to disgorge everything she had swallowed. They turned themselves into green snakes, plunged into Water and swam down to Earth's murky lair. Wind wriggled his coils enticingly, and Earth's fangs gaped as she surged to attack. It took all Wind's speed to keep out of range; but while he distracted Earth's attention Shadow swam silently up behind her, seized her in his python-coils and dragged her spitting and snarling to the surface.

Earth twisted through Water and wriggled through Air, but she was helpless in Shadow's coiling, choking grip. Her struggles tore lumps from her flesh, and they fell into the sea and made islands and continents. Wind and Shadow forced her to disgorge all the creatures she had eaten; then, to prevent her ever preying on living things again, Shadow tore off her lower jaw, fangs and all, and Wind dropped it in the sea, where it formed a jagged underwater reef. Ever since then, Earth has lain subdued (though she still struggles from time to time, crumbling houses like bread-rolls and killing all she can). Most of the disgorged creatures made their homes on Earth, but some chose Air and a few chose Water; one or two went to live in Sun's palace far beyond the stars.

So Wind and Shadow remade creation. But instead of rustling, chattering, singing and twittering, the world's creatures stayed sad and silent, until the lack of noise began to get on Shadow's nerves. "Wind!" he shouted, "What's happened? Why is everything so still?"

Wind answered, "Sun took music away to live

beyond the stars, and creation has been silent ever since."

"Go up there," said Shadow. "Go and fetch music back."

Wind flew up through clouds and chilly air till he reached Sun's palace beyond the stars. It was like a cauldron of blazing fire, and in it Sun sat on a golden throne, while his radiance streamed from him in spears of light. All round him his servants danced and sang. White-dressed girls sang lullabies; sky-blue cloud-herds shepherded their flocks with pan-pipes; drummers in scarlet clothes and head-dresses played war-songs and love-songs; flute-girls in golden dresses played golden flutes.

Although Wind was invisible, Sun still felt the breath of his coming. He whispered to the musicians, "Quick! Stop playing! Hide! Whatever he says, stay away from him. If once he touches you, you'll have to follow him to the silent world below."

At once, without a sound, every musician and dancer in the palace turned into a sun-beam and hid in Sun's fiery sleeve. Wind could see nothing but flames. He hovered for a moment, and his air-currents made the fire-palace roar and gust; then he flew sadly back to Earth.

When Shadow saw Wind empty-handed, he let out a roar of rage which made every creature in the universe cover its ears and cower. Thunder-clouds funnelled into space – and Sun saw their water-drops, panicked, and scuttled like a shooting-star till he plunged into Water and hid there, safe but sizzling. As he fell, the musicians spilled out of his sleeve like sparks, and Wind gathered them, spoke to them gently and floated them down towards Earth.

Wind set the musicians on clouds just above Earth's surface, and dressed himself in a tunic, head-dress and sandals of ceremonial green. His belt was white and gold; gold ornaments jingled on his ears, arms and legs; a rearing serpent crowned his head-dress plumes. He found a mountain-plateau and began to dance, while the Sun's musicians played and sang.

So music returned to Earth, and Wind's dancing carried it to every valley, forest, fold and field. Flowers opened; trees lifted their heads; birds began to sing; soon the whole world was humming, buzzing, chattering and laughing – and has continued to do so ever since. As for Sun, every day at dawn he hears the music and creeps from his underwater hiding-place. All day he soars above the world, enraptured by its sounds; at evening he remembers Shadow's anger, and dives into the sea to hide until next day's music draws him out again.

Amana and her Children

High in the sky, in the star-constellation we call the Pleiades, is a warm blue ocean. Rivers of starlight feed it, and solar winds ruffle its waves; its calms and storms are mirrored in the oceans of the world.

The star-ocean teems with creatures just like those we know on earth: seahorses, flying-fish, anemones, guppies, horseshoe crabs. In weed-forests and on coral hillsides browse a million fish; they skitter like diamonds, and in open water their giant cousins, whale-sharks, marlins and manta-rays, glide among tiny pilot-fish. In other parts of the ocean, like wrecks and reefs on earth, lie jagged rocks, the building-blocks for planets and meteorites. The seabed has stars instead of sand, and in its troughs and chasms volcanoes bubble, thrusting the rock aside and erupting from time to time in constellation-showers across the universe.

The ocean's queen, Amana, has a woman's arms, head and shoulders and a sea-snake's body and tail. Her hair streams in the water like octopus-arms or strands of weed; her skin is white and gold; her serpent-scales are a hundred glitter-ing shades of green. She is forever young: every time her face wrinkles or her scales begin to flake, she sheds her skin like a snake and is reborn more beautiful than before. She rides the seaways on a grey-brown turtle's back, and each day, out of all her subjects, she chooses new companions: a dolphin, a trunk-fish, electric eels, a shoal of yellow-brown pompadour-fish. As she passes, her creatures blow bubbles of delight, and every coral-polyp waves its arms.

At first, when there was nothing in the universe but sun and ocean, Amana lived happily in the sea-kingdom with her creatures. Then, as the undersea volcanoes began tossing planets about the sky, she could not bear to see them bleak and barren, and began clothing them with plants and stocking them with life. Her favourite planet was Earth; she filled it with sea-creatures, modelled on her own ocean-subjects, and covered its continents with soil, trees and plants. She made the seasons to safeguard Earth's fertility, and put clouds and breezes in the sky to blunt the scorching sun.

The sun had been Amana's first creation, long

ago. He had existed in the universe almost as long as she had, and now, when he saw her stocking it with new creations, he was filled with jealousy. As fast as she stocked stars and planets with life, he scorched them dead again; he sent fire-serpents snaking across the sky to swallow Amana's ocean, and they were only defeated when the water quenched their flames and sent them sizzling home. He tried to lick up the Earth in flames, and when Amana's cloud-shield beat him back, he sent heat-worms wriggling through the cracks to parch whatever land they reached.

In the end, Amana felt that even her water-barriers would not prevent the fire-serpents' attacks. She created two champions to protect her kingdom, and gave birth to them in a single day. Her first son, Tamusi, was born in the morning before the day's heat began; her second son, Tamulu, was born in the evening when it was done.

Tamusi and Tamulu were opposites. Tamusi, the morning prince, was a lord of light. He lived in a palace beyond the stars, and his shape was a glitter of silver. Because he was the son of a water-queen, his light was not hot but cold, icy as moonlight on ocean waves. The fire-serpents were no match for it, and each time they attacked Tamusi chopped them to pieces and scattered their remains among the stars. His brother Tamulu, the evening prince, was a lord of darkness. He had no glittering star-palace, no shape,

no wish to be seen at all. Wrapped in shadow-cloaks, he and his goblins sallied out like high-waymen, ambushed the Sun's fire-serpents and smothered them. Tamusi and Tamulu kept out of each other's way, for although they were brothers they were never friends. But they were equals and opposites, and needed each other – for how could light exist without darkness or darkness survive without light?

Thanks to Tamusi and Tamulu, the universe was soon safe from the Sun's attacks. Amana felt that the time had come to create human beings, and place them on Earth to enjoy it. She gave the task of creation to Tamusi, and he made a race of creatures like none ever seen before: they had his mother's head and shoulders, but they had legs to walk on land instead of tails to swim in sea. He carried them gently down to Earth, and they scampered in all directions, exploring. From the sky, the shadow-prince Tamulu watched angrily. He was jealous of his brother – why had he, too, not been entrusted with making the human race? He created beings of his own – monsters, shadow-spirits, phantoms – and hid them on Earth to plague his brother's human race. This is why at night, when Tamusi turns away from Earth, darkness and terror rule; only when the morning star rises and daylight floods the sky is the human race safe in Tamusi's protection, able to bustle about its business and enjoy the teeming world its ancestor Amana made for it.

Under-earth, Over-earth

AUSTRALIA : TIWI PEOPLE OF MELVILLE ISLAND

On the shores of Australia's Northern Territory is a gaunt sea-inlet called Van Diemen Gulf. Beside it lie two enormous islands. Nowadays the islands are fertile, shaggy with trees and full of the rustle of birds, insects and animals. But in the Dream Time, at the beginning of the world, nothing lived on them. They were part of the mainland then, and like the rest of the mainland they were a mud-wilderness, flat and treeless. No sun shone, no moon; nothing stirred.

Although over-earth was dead and bare, life existed in under-earth. Mudungkala, Mother of All, lived there with her two daughters and her son. Under-earth was dark and empty, and no sounds broke its silence but the tiny chuckles of Mudungkala's children as they played at her feet, and her own sighs at the blackness and boredom of the world she lived in. At last she grew tired of it. She gathered her wriggling children and stood up till her shoulders pressed hard against the clay-ceiling above her head. The earth shook and roared, and showers of mud fell down. Then, when Mudungkala's strength was almost done

and she felt she could push no more, the clay-canopy split apart, and she squeezed out into over-earth with her children in her arms.

Mudungkala fell on hands and knees, and while her children clung to her, crawled east, west, north and south, following the four winds. Everywhere she went she parted the land behind her, leaving a channel which the sea curled hungrily in to fill. Soon an island was formed, and Mudungkala put her children gently down on it and said, "This new land is yours. Live and prosper here forever."

In endless darkness, the children could see nothing. But as they sat on the cold, bare earth, sniffing the air, they suddenly felt life stirring all round them. Mudungkala was making creatures to live with them in over-earth: hawks, pigeons, kookaburras, parakeets, chipmunks, kangaroos, gazelles, mice, men, lions, koalas, otters, women, lizards, snakes, wasps, dragon-flies, anteaters, grasshoppers, fleas, everything that has ever existed or ever will exist in earth or sky or sea. The air filled with chirping, rustling and whispering. The children were frightened: they wailed, held

out their arms and turned their faces this way and that in the darkness to find their mother. But Mudungkala had vanished. As soon as creation was finished, she disappeared and was never seen on over-earth again.

Time passed. The children grew up and had children of their own. The animals, birds and other creatures prospered. Bare over-earth grew a covering of trees, bushes, grass and shrubs. The only thing left of under-earth was darkness: sightlessly, the creatures picked their way through the island's forests and wandered across its plains. Some even blundered into the sea and drowned.

One day Jurumu and Mudati, Mudungkala's grandsons, were sitting talking in the dark forest. As they talked, Jurumu rubbed two pieces of stick together – and they began to smoke, and glowed hotter and hotter until they burned his hands. He threw them down, and they landed in a heap of leaves and twigs and set it blazing with sudden light. It was the first fire ever seen in the world – and its brightness dazzled the eyes of Jurumu, Mudati and the forest creatures round about, and filled them with terror.

What were Jurumu and Mudati to do? How could they kill the terrifying new creature they had made? They ran to their grandfather, the boy-child Mudungkala had once carried up from under-earth. "You've discovered fire," he said. "Don't kill it. Keep it alive, and let it warm you, protect you and heat food for you."

He showed them how to feed the flames with sticks and logs. Gradually, as Jurumu and Mudati learned to control fire, they lost their fear of it. But the other creatures of over-earth stayed shy of its flames and heat. They left it for the men's plaything, kept well clear of it and watched it with wary eyes.

So fire became the servant of humans, not of animals, and they used it to dominate all other creatures. They used it to dominate darkness too. One of the first things Jurumu's and Mudati's grandfather told them to do was to light two blazing torches and give them to their grand-mothers, his sisters, Mudungkala's girl-babies from under-earth long ago. The old women soared into the sky, and from that day to this their torches have filled heaven and earth with light. The older daughter's torch is as yellow as fire, and she calls it Sun; the younger daughter's torch is as silver as the sea, and she calls it Moon.

How Light Became

The first beings were Mother Earth and Father Sky. They were so passionately in love, and clung so tightly together, that there was not so much as a chink of light between them.

Six beings lived in the darkness between Earth and Sky. They were their children, and their names were Father of Fields, Father of Forests, Father of Hedgerows, Father of Heroes, Father of Seas and Father of Winds. They were proud princes, and it hurt their pride to live squashed and cramped between their parents.

"We must put an end to it," said Father of Hedgerows.

"How?"

"We must make them separate, make them give us room and light."

"No!" shouted Father of Winds. "They love each other. Why should they separate just for us? Leave them as they are."

The others ignored him. They bent their minds to ways of making their parents separate.

Father of Fields said, "I think I have it. Let me try." He began talking to Earth and Sky in a dignified, reasonable voice. He was as unhurried as the ripening of summer crops, and he gave Earth and Sky a hundred reasons why they should separate and give their children light. Unfortunately, the more he talked the more Father of Winds howled and roared, until in the end his storming drowned every word Father of Fields was trying to say.

At last Father of Fields was too hoarse to say any more. "Words are useless," said Father of Hedgerows. "Let me try something else." In the folds of his robe he had a hundred scurrying mammals, a thousand birds and a million insects – all the wild creatures that would one day live in hedgerows across the world. He took them out in handfuls and whispered his message to them, and they buzzed, squeaked and twittered away to pass it on to Earth and Sky. But before the cloud of them dispersed, Father of Winds puffed out his cheeks and blew a blast that sent them scattering back to safety in Father of Hedgerow's robes.

"It's no use sending creatures," said Father of Seas. "Let me try something else." He stirred all his waves and waters together, and began pouring them into the crevices between Earth and Sky. His idea was to let the water-level rise gradually and slowly, until his parents floated apart without even noticing. But Father of Winds again blew an enormous blast and spilled the waters in a tidal wave over the edge of Earth's body, till she and Sky floated in a placid ocean, peaceful as babes in a boat and embracing as tightly as before.

"This is all wasted effort," said Father of Heroes. "Let me try something else." He crawled to a space in the darkness where he could stand upright. Then he planted his feet wide apart, brandished his spear, shook his fist, stamped his feet and shouted threats of what would happen unless Earth and Sky unwrapped themselves. Father of Winds sent a breeze snaking between his legs, and it caught him off balance and sent him sprawling, threats and all.

"There's only one way left," said Father of Forests. "Let me try." He lay on his back, flat on Mother Earth, and braced his shoulders. Then he lifted his legs, set his feet against Father Sky and began to heave. Earth and Sky clutched each other as tightly as if they were one single flesh. Father of Winds fretted and gusted round Father of Forest's legs, trying to dislodge them. But Father of Forests knew that only trees which resist a storm are broken; those that bend survive. He twisted his legs this way and that, countering even Father of Wind's fiercest gusts, and at the same time he let his limbs grow slowly upwards, powerful and slow as trees. There was a crack, a groan, a split, and Earth and Sky came apart at last and Sky flew spinning overhead.

Light flooded into the space between Earth and Sky, and Father of Forests sat up and relaxed his limbs, while four of his brothers lifted their arms and cheered. Only the fifth of them, Father of Winds, had no rejoicing. He looked at Mother Earth's broken body, already changing in the daylight to hills and grassy plains, and at her tears streaming to make a broad, flowing river. He looked at Father Sky, spreadeagled and helpless far above. Then he knelt by Mother Earth's weeping head, bunched his fists and swore unending war on his brothers and all their creatures, war that would rage in thunderstorms and hurricanes till the end of time.

Seven Days

MIDDLE EAST (THE BIBLE)

Before creation began, there was a water-desert. It was shapeless, deep and dark. No tides or currents stirred it; no winds ruffled its surface; it was neither hot nor cold. Nothing lived in it or disturbed its emptiness; the only thing that moved across its surface was the spirit of God.

On the first day of creation, God formed his spirit into words and said, "Let there be light." At once light appeared, shining from the flat water far into the gulf of space. God separated it from darkness, and called the light Day and the darkness Night. When it was finished and he was satisfied, the first day was done.

On the second day God said, "Let there be sky," and sky appeared. It was made from water and shared water's nature. But water was heavy with the weight of darkness and stayed below; sky was alive with light and soared above. God called the sky Heaven, and when it was set in place and he was satisfied, the second day was done.

On the third day God said, "Let there be land." He gathered together all the water under heaven and formed it into pools. Wherever the water-level sank, dry land appeared. God fixed water and land forever in their places, and called the water Sea and the dry land Earth. He covered Earth with plants. On the mountains and hillsides, where the air was cold and the soil was thin, he planted mosses, lichens and brightly-coloured alpine flowers. Lower down he planted pine-trees, firs, bracken, brambles, wild roses, nettles, honey-suckle, rhododendron and a thousand other trees and shrubs. On the plains, where the soil was thick and fertile, he planted oats, barley, narcissus, gladiolus, celandine, wild cherries, almonds, willows, palms, horse-chestnuts, poppies, roots and vegetables of every kind. He made even deserts and sandy beaches flower: wherever there was a speck of moisture cactus, thistles and dune-grass took their place. As soon as he made each plant, God gave it seeds to recreate itself. He made Earth a fertile garden, and began its cycle of growth and seedtime, seedtime and unending growth. In the evening he walked in the garden, and when he was satisfied with everything he had made, the third day was done.

On the fourth day God said, "Let there be stars." He picked up all the light he had made on the first day of creation and scattered it across the sky. Some fell in large, single drops like the Evening Star; the rest splashed across Heaven's floor in constellations and galaxies like the Milky Way. God separated the two brightest lights from all the others and called them Sun and Moon. Sun rules the day and Moon the night, and their rising and setting control all times and seasons on the Earth. When the sun, moon and stars were made and God was satisfied, the fourth day was done.

On the fifth day God said, "Let there be creatures in sea and air." He stocked the sea with fish: sharks, anchovies, swordfish, octopus, herring, coelocanths, squid, codfish, conger eels; he filled the air with insects, and set birds hovering in the sky and darting from tree to tree. He made albatrosses and gulls to skim the sea, and gannets, cormorants and pelicans to plunge into it; he made plovers and swifts to sweep across the Earth, and condors, falcons and eagles to soar in the air above. To live in fresh water he made ducks, herons, moorhens, swans; he made parrots, toucans, weaver-birds, parakeets and cockatoos to perch in trees, and woodpeckers, nuthatches, cranes and rooks to nest in them. As he had with plants, he gave all these creatures the power to recreate themselves, and when he was satisfied with everything he had made, the fifth day was done.

On the sixth day God said, "Let there be landcreatures." One by one he visited all the regions of the Earth, and stocked them with the animals most suited to their climate and their plants. For the polar ice-caps in the north and south he made arctic foxes, walruses and polar bears; for deserts he made gerbils, lizards and rattle-snakes; he gave monkeys, flying-foxes, boa-constrictors and ant-eaters jungle homes, and filled the plains with elephants, giraffes, rhinoceroses and buffaloes, as well as zebras and wildebeeste and the lions, hyenas and cheetahs that prey on them. He made grazing animals, cattle, deer, goats and sheep; he made dogs, cats, squirrels, frogs, hippos, chameleons, vipers, rabbits, pigs, wallabies, coatimundis, lynxes, dormice, pangolins, bats and snails. Last of all he made two human beings, a man and a woman, and gave them power over every other creature on land, sea or air. When God was satisfied with all the animals he had made, and with the coming of humankind, the sixth day was done.

So in six days God created light, heaven, sea, air, earth and everything that lives or breathes in them. On the seventh day, when everything was set in order and the universe was complete, he rested.

Giants and Gods

NORTHERN EUROPE : THE VIKINGS

In the north was a desert of frost and ice, jagged outcrops splintered across frozen snow. The season was winter; the time was twilight; the weather was blizzard. The south, by contrast, blazed like a blacksmith's forge. The ground bled rock; sparks showered; the sky flared fire.

In between north and south was the gap of space. At first nothing could cross it, neither northern chill nor southern fire. But as the southern volcanoes spat sparks higher and further, a rain of hot ash began to waft down on the ice-floes of the north. The ice thawed and dripped – and out of the drips Ymir, first of the giants, was formed, and a host of smaller giants grew from his sweat-drops as he lay soaking in the heat.

While Ymir sweltered, the giantlings swarmed across the ice-plains like termites. They ripped the rocks apart to build castles; they churned the snow to slush with their dancing and their singing filled the fog. The north suddenly became a clumping, crowded place.

In the midst of all the racket, the melting ice formed another being: Audumla, a black-skinned, brown-eyed cow. As soon as they saw her the giantlings fell on her with whoops of joy, clamped thirsty lips to her udders and drank her milk, jostling and sucking till not a drop was left. Then they cartwheeled back to their games, leaving her exhausted, alone and starving.

Audumla plodded across the snow-fields looking for pasture. The southern sky was rosy with reflected fire; the frost-blue northern sky rumbled with the giantlings' games. The horizon was ice-hills; the foreground was water; there was no grass. In the end, desperate for nourishment, Audumla began licking the salty ice – and as she licked the ice gradually took on warrior-form, as if a fighter had been sleeping there, waiting to be released. His name was Buri, and as soon as he slipped free of the ice he married a giantess and produced a family of warrior-gods. They colonised the plains, built fortresses and settlements, and were soon as numerous and noisy as the giants themselves.

So things stood in the universe. On one side were giants, on the other were gods, and they hated each other and coveted each others' living-space. There were fights and arguments, but neither side had strength enough to outmatch the other. Then three god-brothers, led by Odin, put an end to it. Instead of attacking the giantlings (who outnumbered them) they crept up on aged Ymir and cut him to death with knives. Ymir's blood – salt water, like that of all giants – poured from him in a flood which drowned his giantling children and made the first ocean; when his body was drained the gods tipped it into the space between north and south and used it to make the world. From his flesh they made earth, and planted in it the hairs of his head for trees; they built his bones into mountains, and hung up his skull to make the sky, filling it with sparks for sun and stars.

But although the gods' triumph made them masters of the universe, they were not the only beings left alive in it. Two giantlings had escaped from the flood of Ymir's blood which drowned their relatives; now they hid on high ground among the northern ice-hills, and set about breeding a new race of giants to destroy the gods. And from the maggots which swarmed in Ymir's murdered flesh, a race of trolls was born. The gods scooped them up and crammed them underground – and they scurried about in caverns and crevices, plotting revenge on the gods for depriving them of light.

The gods were afraid of the new giants and trolls, and of the revenge they might one day take. So they built a fortress, high in space, to keep them out. They made its walls of mountain-sides, cemented them with ice and hedged them with Ymir's eyebrows. They built a rainbow-bridge to lead from their new kingdom to the earth below. They called the kingdom Asgard, and when it was finished they began moving all their goods, chattels and families to settle there in safety. Before they left the earth, there was one more thing to do. They took an ash-tree and a vine, and transformed them into the first man and the first woman ever created. Their names were Ask and Embla, and they and their descendants have lived ever afterwards as the gods' caretakers here on earth, farming it, repairing the damage done by giants or trolls, and keeping it green and fertile in case the gods come visiting.

The Streams of Life

NIGERIA : THE IJAW PEOPLE

For a thousand ages the world knew no weather but thunderstorms. Lightning crackled; thunder growled; rain pelted like iron. Then, in a single moment, the weather entirely changed. Rain and thunder vanished; the sun blazed down from a cloudless sky. Its heat began to dry the sodden earth. The mud steamed and split apart to make hills and a dusty plain. And on the plain, where nothing had been before, three objects appeared: a table, a chair and the flat creation-stone.

Stone, chair and table lay unused for generations. There were no people in the world – and if there had been, they would have been too small to use objects so enormous: it would have been like termites trying to pull a plough. Then one day, as unexpectedly as the change had been before from rain to sun, there was another rumble of thunder, and Mother Woyengi stepped down in a lightning-flash from sky to earth.

Woyengi burrowed in the ground, heaving aside the surface dust and scooping up handfuls of the damp, dark-brown earth below. She dumped it on the table, sat down on the chair and rested her feet on the creation-stone. Then, quickly before the earth could dry in the sun, she began shaping it into dolls. As she finished each one, she lifted it to her nostrils and gave it the breath of life.

By the time Woyengi had used up all the earth, the table-top swarmed with doll-people. They wriggled and squirmed, and their piping filled the air. They were brown and naked, with blind, closed eyes and spindly limbs. They had no sex, and no clothes. One by one Woyengi picked them up, gently smoothed their eyes open with her fingers, and whispered in their ears, "You can choose to be a man or a woman for the rest of your life. Which is it to be?" One by one the doll-people chose, and Woyengi dressed the women in plain white dresses and the men in plain white shirts and set them back down on the table-top. This time, instead of piping and wriggling, they sat gazing round with their new bright eyes, talking eagerly or peering over the table-edges at the world below.

When Woyengi had dressed all her children, she spoke to them again, and at the sound of her voice every movement on the table-top ended and

everyone stood still to hear. "Your first gift was life," she said, "and your second gift was sex. For your third gift, you can choose the kind of existence you want to live on earth."

At once a babble of voices rose from the doll-people. "I want a dozen children!" "Give me a big house!" "Make me wise!" "Let me be fearless!" "Help me make music!" "Teach me to heal the sick!" Woyengi waited till every one of them was finished, then stretched out her arms and said, "As you've chosen, so it is. Your wishes are granted."

As she spoke these words, the new witch-doctors, wise-women, carpenters, sailors, farmers, potters, washerwomen, musicians, fishermen, chiefs, princesses, weavers, hunters, bakers and mothers-of-families-to-be felt power and character stream into them. Gathered on a table-top in the middle of a dust-plain, the whole human race began laughing, chattering, shouting, linking arms, singing and dancing. It was the first day of life, the first gathering of humanity and the world's first party, all in one.

As the happy noise continued, Woyengi began picking her children up in handfuls. She stepped down from the creation-stone and carried them away from the table to another part of the plain. Here there were two blue streams, rippling across the plain as far as the horizon. Woyengi knelt on the ground between the streams, and set her people down. She said, "The stream on this side leads to luxury; the stream on that side leads to ordinariness. You've chosen the kind of life you want; go to the proper stream, and let its water carry you where you chose to be."

The human beings looked at the two streams. Both shimmered placidly in the sunlight. But when the people who had asked for riches, fame or power stepped into their stream, they found it fast-flowing and dangerous with weeds and currents. The people who had asked for humble, helpful or creative lives stepped into the other stream and found it shallow, clean and clear. Both sides shouted back their discoveries, and several of the people still on shore began to draw timidly back from the water and ask Woyengi if there was time to change their minds. Sternly she shook her head. The life they had chosen on the table-top was fixed forever: they had no choice now but to go to it.

So, one after another, Woyengi's children began floating or swimming in the stream of riches and the stream of ordinariness, and the waters carried them away and began to irrigate the world with the human race.

The First Made Man

NORTH AMERICA : TEWA INDIANS

The world began in a swirl of mud, water and choking mist. At first there was no dry land, but the churning water spat mud-balls higher and higher, and they settled gradually into continents. The ground oozed, fit to grow nothing but green bog-moss. A few light-footed animals lived there, feeding on one another; overhead only birds of prey braved the cold, wet air.

While the world slithered and settled above their heads, human beings waited underground, in slimy caverns under a broad, deep lake. A steep tunnel led to the surface; its walls dripped slime, stalactites hung from its roof like knives, and there was no sound in it but the trickle of water to stagnant pools far below. No humans dared climb the tunnel; they huddled in their caverns and waited till the world above was dry. Their twin rulers were Summer Mother and Winter Mother. No one yet knew what summer and winter were; all they saw was that growth and fertility filled Summer Mother's cave, while Winter Mother's people shivered among snow-banks and ice-rimmed water-pools. Warm-blooded creatures, quails, marmosets, wood-mice, zebras, stags, nestled in Summer Mother's arms; Winter Mother's servants were polar bears, seals, terns and shoals of pale-eyed, nameless fish.

From time to time, as the seas and continents formed overhead, Summer Mother and Winter Mother sent a man up the tunnel to scout the surface and bring back news of what he saw. The first time there was nothing but mud and dark; the second time he talked of reeds and of stars in distant clouds; the third time he told of blue sky glimpsed among the mists; the fourth time he reported green moss-plains rolling to the horizon. But each time, when Summer Mother and Winter Mother asked if the world was ripe yet for humans, he answered, "No."

After the man's fourth journey Summer Mother and Winter Mother said, "You must go further up. You could have seen everything you tell us about, stars, blue sky, reeds and plains, without once stepping outside the tunnel. Go higher; climb the banks of the lake; keep going till you reach ground that bears your weight."

Wearily the man began to climb the slippery tunnel yet again. His bare feet slithered on the rocks, he splashed through pools and grazed his skin on stalactites. At last he saw a window of light at the tunnel's end, and finally reached the surface. Trembling with terror, he stepped clear of the tunnel, waded through reedbeds and crept over boggy ground, until he felt firm grass underfoot and flung himself down to rest.

No sooner was he lying there than a group of predators ran up: a fox, a coyote, a bobcat, a wolf, a crow, a vulture, and a mountain-lion. Screeching and howling, they fell on him and began ripping his flesh. He was too exhausted to defend himself, and lay still – and at once, to his astonishment, the animals and birds drew back, and his wounds scarred over in an instant as if they had never been.

"Well done!" purred Mountain-lion. "You've passed the test of bravery. From now on, animals will accept human beings and allow them to share the world."

While Mountain-lion and Man waited on the grass, the other animals and birds fetched presents. Vulture brought arrows, and Wolf a painted quiver to put them in. Coyote brought a bow, and Fox black face-paint in a bowl. Last of all, Bobcat brought three feathers for the man's hair, and two crows held up an embroidered hunting-coat.

"Take these," said Mountain-lion. "Wear the coat and feathers, paint your face, and carry the bow and arrows to the underworld. You are the First Made Man, the Hunt Chief who will lead and care for your people. Go down, and tell them the world is ripe."

So the First Made Man went back down the long tunnel to his people, and this time instead of creeping he ran boldly along, sure-footed as a hunter. As he ran he gave short, brisk fox's yelps to tell the others he was coming. Summer Mother and Winter Mother gathered all the people, and told the First Made Man to lead them to the upper world. As the long column of humans picked its way up the tunnel towards the light, some of them faltered, and Summer Mother encouraged them with prophecies of planting and harvest, and sowed soft grass to ease their steps. Others scrabbled for finger-holds in the slimy walls, and Winter Mother touched the dampness with her sleeve, and froze it to stone-stiff ice.

At last the straggling line reached daylight, and the First Made Man led them to firm ground and told them to build a settlement. They stayed there for several seasons, while the world dried; then they split into two groups and went separate ways. Farmers and gatherers followed Summer Mother to cultivate the rolling plains; hunters and fishermen followed Winter Mother, and made their homes in mountains and beside the snarling sea. As for the First Made Man, the Hunt Chief, he stayed where he was, at home with the animals and birds who had first accepted him and welcomed the human race to share their world.

Fire-lords

At first there was no light, darkness, land, air, sun or space: nothing but a formless gulf called Chaos. Scattered everywhere, like dust-specks, were the beginnings of the universe. Gradually, as Chaos swirled round them, the specks began huddling together – and so the first shapes of things were made. Dark and Light took half of Chaos each for their kingdoms, and each produced children. Dark's children were Dreams, Sleep and Death; Light's children were Stars, Comets and Love soaring on golden wings.

Two other shapes of emptiness, Earth and Sky, were filled with the glow of Love, and began to people the universe with children. First, for Earth, they made rocks, seas, plants and trees; then, for Sky, they made clouds, winds, rain and sun. Next they blended parts of their new creation and made giants. The first three were a blend of rock and trees: they had stony bodies, a hundred branching arms, twig-fingers and bark-skin. The second three, called "Round-eyes" or Cyclopes, blended the sun's heat with earth and air: they had four limbs, stocky bodies and heads with noses, mouths and round, single eyes.

Sky hated his children. He loathed the hundred-handed monsters, and shuddered at the hill-high, one-eyed Cyclopes. They covered their two lower limbs with leather shoes, and their upper limbs held round discs and pointed sticks – why? Their single eyes gazed watchfully all round, as if for enemies – but what enemies had they in an empty universe? Sky was baffled, and his bafflement made him afraid.

When Earth's next children, the twelve Titans, were born, they were even less like their father Sky. They had alert minds, graceful bodies and gentle, harmonious movements. Sky looked at them, sprawling helplessly on the surface of Mother Earth, and his temper overflowed. He roared down on Earth in a savage storm, prised her rocky body apart and levered every one of her children inside, out of sight and out of mind.

Earth lay in agony. Her body was gouged and split. Deep down lay the Hundred-handed monsters, like rock-piles sulking far underground. Above them the Cyclopes set up blacksmiths'

forges, and there worked the fire they had inherited from Sky, until the heat scorched her bones and blistered her rocky flesh. Near the surface the twelve youngest children whimpered and waved their arms.

There was no way for Earth to take revenge. Long ago, when Sky chose movement as his wedding-gift, she had chosen bulk. Now all she could do was wallow while her husband raged and roared above her just as he pleased. Long centuries passed, and every so often he remembered his fury, swooped down and burnt her black with sun or tore her apart with storms.

At last, Earth could bear no more. Her older children, the Hundred-handed giants and the Cyclopes, were buried too deep to help her. But she whispered to Kronos, the quickest-witted of all her Titan children, a way to take revenge. He took a sickle, made from flint studded with sharp-edged diamonds, and lay in wait till his father Sky next attacked. Then he leapt out of hiding, lifted the sickle and hacked at Sky's body high above his head. There was a blaze of agony, a hiss of light, and Sky flew clear of Earth forever.

One by one Kronos' brothers and sisters, the other Titans, crept out on to the surface of Mother Earth. They blinked in the light, and stared with delight at their new kingdom. They divided it between them: some took the seas to rule, others the hills and plains of Earth, others the vault of Space. They soared and swam and sang; the universe was their playground; everything in it existed for their delight.

In their excitement, the Titans utterly forgot their monster-relatives. The three Hundred-handed giants lay in their prison, deep in Earth's secret heart. They had no intelligence to understand what had happened, but they knew that the Titans had cheated them, and they skulked in the darkness dreaming of revenge. As for the blacksmith-Cyclopes, they had a gift owned by no other children of Earth and Sky: they owned fire, and the knowledge it brought. They knew that one day the Titans themselves would have children, Zeus and the other gods, and that those children would fight them to control the universe. When that fight came, the Cyclopes meant to give Zeus all-conquering fire, stored in thunderbolts. Fire would help him rout the Titans and rule creation – and the Cyclopes' revenge on the Titans would be complete.

Old-spider and her Helpers

In the darkness before creation, Old-spider lived alone. So far as she knew, there were no other living creatures; even so she hung a web from the corners of darkness to trap any that came her way. But nothing stirred; the web hung empty. From time to time, Old-spider ate it, rewove it and hung it up again; apart from that, she went hungry.

After many hungry ages, Old-spider decided not to wait for prey, but to hunt for it. Dangling from a safety-thread, she felt her way into every cranny and corner of the darkness, her senses alert for the slightest quiver of life. She went east, north and west and found nothing but emptiness on every side. It was only when she extended the lifeline and began exploring south, that her long front legs at last struck something hard. Prey! She bunched her legs round it and tried to stun it with her poison-fangs. But the fangs flattened uselessly against the prey's hard shell, and sent pain stinging through Old-spider's every nerve.

What could the object be? She felt it all over, and could find no clue. It was like an enormous, corrugated stone. But its smell was alive and warm, and when she tapped it, instead of giving back a stone's dry click it echoed like a drum. "Whatever this is," Old-spider thought, "It's hollow – and if it's hollow I can get inside."

All spiders possess charms and hypnotic powers – and Old-spider, mother of all, possessed all the magic of the universe. She charmed the hollow object – it was a giant clam – with an opening-spell, and its halves hinged apart just wide enough for her to dart inside and bundle her legs quickly after her before the shell snapped shut.

Now, instead of hanging outside in empty dark, Old-spider lay tangled in the clam's equally dark inside. Warm, wet flesh pressed against her; she could see nothing, and she was cramped and cross. As she felt around, her foot touched a second hard-shelled object. This time it was a snail, tiny and timid, which had long ago slid inside the clam and been engulfed. As soon as she felt it, Old-spider made a plan. She could have stunned the snail and sucked it dry; instead, she rolled it in spider-silk, cradled it in the crook of a leg, and willed herself and it into a magic sleep.

When they woke up, some of Old-spider's magic had passed into the snail, and she uncoiled the silk and set it free. She said, "Little snail, little snail, will you prise this clam-shell open, and give me room to stretch?" The snail slid to the place where the clam-shells joined, and began to force itself in between. The clam responded by clamping its jaws even tighter, and the little snail had to exert all its new magic force to prise the shell apart. As it moved around, trying foothold after foothold, it left a phosphorescent trail, and the clam's flesh began to glow with dim, silvery light.

At last the clam relaxed its jaws to make room for the little snail. The shells gripped the snail like pincers, but now there was space for Old-spider to move about, and a glimmer of snail-light to see by – and the first things she saw were two more creatures, another snail and a worm coiled in the centre of the clam-shell.

"Wake up, wake up," whispered Old-spider. "There's work to do. The clam's not open yet. Wake up and help!"

As soon as the spell reached them, the creatures woke. The snail saw the silver light her brother had made, and began to match it with a golden, bright-shining light-trail of her own. The worm – whose name was Rigi – uncoiled himself and wriggled to the opening in the clam-shell. He set his head against the upper shell and his tail against the lower, and heaved. The clam knew that if its shell was ever prised fully open it would die, and resisted with all its might. Time after time Rigi forced the jaws apart, only to have them press down again as fiercely as before. Sweat poured from him and slopped in the clam's lower shell.

As the struggle continued, Rigi's sweat-puddle turned into a pool, the pool into a lake, the lake into a sea and the sea into an ocean which filled the clam's body and choked its flesh with saltiness. All at once, with a heave of agony, the shell snapped open and the clam lay dead. Rigi's sweat-ocean spilled over the lower shell and made a wide, deep sea.

Old-spider made the lower clam-shell World and the upper clam-shell Sky. She lifted the two snails high in the sky-shell, and called them Moon and Sun. They took it in turns to light the world below: while silver Moon stood on guard, Sun rolled round the clam-shell to rest in the sea; when golden Sun rose up, Moon sank down to rest. From that moment on, sky, sea, the clam-shell and everything in it were filled with light, and the darkness that had been there before creation disappeared forever. From the clam's flesh Old-spider made islands, and dressed them in lush green grass.

When that part of creation was finished, Old-spider turned to Rigi – and found him drowned in the sea of his own sweat. The effort of prising the clam apart had been too much for him. Old-spider wrapped his body in a silk cocoon, carried it back up her anchor-thread, laid it to rest across the sky, and made it the star-web we call the Milky Way.

The Five Sisters

Everything began with water, a glass-smooth sea filling the universe from edge to edge. Above it floated a cloud, and on the cloud lived Old One.

Old One was Chief of the universe. But he was also the only being in existence, and had no company but his own. He amused himself by taking long walks across the springy cloud, or by lying on his stomach watching his reflection in the sea below. He shouted and sang, till echoes filled the universe.

After a thousand ages, Old One grew bored with echoes, reflections and cloud-walks. He decided to make a world, to create land in the sea and fill it with teeming, fascinating life.

First, Old One converted his airy cloud into a heavy fogbank, hovering just above the sea. Then he plucked five hairs from his beard and planted them in the fog like seedlings. He sprinkled them with sea-water, and they grew into five tall, beautiful girls. Old One took the first of them aside and asked her, "Is there anything in the world you'd like to be?"

She answered, "I'd like to be Earth, fruitful and fertile, the home of life."

"So you shall be," he said. "You can nourish growing seeds, and give food and shelter to living things. When they die, you can take them in your arms and cradle them forever. Your children will be plants, flowers and animals of every kind."

Then Old One took his second daughter aside and asked her, "Is there anything in the world you'd like to be?"

She answered, "I'd like to be Water, rippling everywhere across the Earth."

"So you shall be," he said. "Every plant and animal on Earth will drink life from you, and your children will be water-plants, crustaceans and fish of every kind."

Then Old One took his third daughter aside and asked her, "Is there anything in the world you'd like to be?"

She answered, "I'd like to be Fire, blazing everywhere, bringing all Earth's creatures light and warmth."

"So you shall be," said Old One. "Your home

will be in flints, logs, tree-bark, twigs and grass. Your light will be reflected in the sun, moon and stars. Your children will be lizards, salamanders, snakes and insects of every kind.''

Fire went to join her sisters Earth and Water on the fogbank's edge. When they were all ready, Earth somersaulted from the fogbank to the sea, and at once changed into continents, plains and hills. Her every fold filled with life: trees, flowers, bracken, lichen, moss and a myriad browsing, burrowing animals.

As soon as Earth was formed, Water and Fire dived to join her. Water fell to Earth in a shower of droplets, and made rivers, pools and lakes in every cranny. She gurgled into the sea and stirred it into life; wherever she went she left children: mussels, sea-urchins, frogs, newts, daphnia, waterboatmen and a myriad silver fish, from sticklebacks to dolphins, from herring to hump-back whales. Fire fell to Earth in a lightning-flash, and buried herself deep in hollow caves, coursing in red-hot lava to the surface. Her sparks settled in twigs and dry leaves, waiting to be discovered; in the sky above she left pieces of herself, the sun, moon and stars, to warm Earth's creatures; her lizards, snakes and insect-children hid in crevices, basked on warm, flat rocks or began buzzing from plant to plant.

While all this was happening, Old One and his two remaining daughters watched from the fogbank. Old One asked his fourth daughter, "Is there anything in the world you'd like to be?"

She answered, "I'd like to be the mother of men and women. My children will be wise and kind, and will live on Earth in peace and harmony."

"Rubbish!" said her sister. "*I* shall be mother of the human race. My children will be strong, cunning and pitiless, and will make slaves of all the other creatures in the world."

Old One sighed. "So be it," he said. "You've both chosen, and your wishes are granted. From now on, you'll live on your sister Earth, and Fire and Water will nourish your children and give them life. There will be good people and bad people, and the world will be full of murder, battle and misery. But I have one present left: the gift of hope. One day, after long centuries of suffering, good will triumph and bad will disappear from Earth forever. So I promise, and so it will be."

He leaned on his stick and helped his daughters step down from the fogbank to the surface of Earth. Then he soared into the sky and was never seen again. Creation was finished, and humanity's long life began.

Ra

EGYPT

In the sea that was there before the world, a single, perfect flower appeared. It was a lotus. It had a green stem, flat waxy leaves, and milk-white petals folded like a fist. The lotus-bud bobbed on the water in the darkness, and inside, safe as a child in its mother's womb, slept the baby sun.

The sun's name was Ra, and he and the lotus were the only living things. As the lotus-bud fattened, so baby Ra inside it slept and grew, dribbling, sucking his chubby fingers and waiting to be born.

Most flowers unfold in the daytime, opening their petals to the life-giving light. But the lotus prefers darkness: it stays shut all through the day's brightness, and opens each evening to drink the dark. So it was with the lotus that was Ra's cradle, floating in the darkness before time began. One by one its petals uncurled and spread until it lay fully open, bobbing on the sea like a saucer. As it opened, it filled the darkness with the first — and sweetest — flower-scent the universe has ever known. The scent tickled baby Ra's nostrils and woke him up. He stretched his arms and legs and opened his eyes — and at once dazzling sunlight streamed out of them and sent the sea-spray skittering.

In the instant he was born, Ra grew to full maturity. One second there was a chubby baby gurgling in a lotus, the next a grown prince towering from horizon to horizon. He imagined children and grandchildren, and they too immediately appeared: Air, Rain and Sky above the sea, and Earth scattered across it from side to side.

As Ra soared above the sea, looking down at his new creation, the dazzle of his own sunbeams glittered back at him from a thousand waves. The glare made his eyes water, and the water-drops fell to earth and turned into insects, fish, birds, animals and human beings, shaking their bodies to dislodge the golden drops.

So the world's creatures were born from tears, and tears and sorrow have been their nature ever since. They are restless, fierce and cruel; they are forever preying on each other; they take more pleasure in arguing than in all the riches of creation spread around them.

Of all the world's creatures, human beings were the most unruly. Their arrogance grew like a weed; they hurt or enslaved everything else on earth. They bickered among themselves, and laughed at Ra and the other gods. In the end, Ra lost his temper, plucked out one of his eyes and hurled it to destroy them. The golden eye hurtled across the earth like a fiery stone, parching the ground, scorching the crops and devastating the human race with plague. Dead bodies lay everywhere, and their stench rose up and poisoned the air.

But without his eye Ra quickly grew feeble. Before long he was old and toothless, and his mouth drooled and dribbled as it had when he was a child. Half-blind, he blundered in water-caverns in the underworld; he no longer had enough strength to stand up tall and send life-giving light across the world. Darkness ruled; the few mortals left alive on earth covered their faces and wept.

At this point Ra's children and grand-children, the other gods, decided to take a hand. Air and Earth lay down, flat on the ground, and Sky placed herself face-down on top of them. She stretched out till her toes and fingers touched the horizon in the east and in the west. Then slowly, with enormous effort, she began arching her back, lifting herself on toes and fingers into a bent-bow shape. The effort locked her muscles stone-hard with cramp; the blood ran out of them until she was fixed in place for all eternity, unable ever to move again. As she hung there, propped on finger-tips and toes, Air stood up and held out his hands, palms upwards, to support her, and Earth smoothed the rotting bodies from his kingdom and made the ground green and fertile once again.

From that moment on, Ra begins each day at the place where Sky's finger-tips touch the eastern horizon. He is twisted and haggard after his journey through the underworld. But while he has been away from the earth, the lotus which cradled him as a baby has bloomed in the darkness, and filled the upper world with scent. Ra draws youth and strength from its perfume, as he did at the start of creation, and begins to travel the sky, clambering along the arch of Sky's body. The journey takes twelve hours, and while it lasts he surveys his mortal subjects below, and sends light to help the good and heat and drought to parch the bad. By evening, when he reaches Sky's toes on the western horizon, he is once more old and bent, and has strength only to step into a silver boat which will carry him through the sea-caves of the underworld, till he breathes the lotus-perfume once more next morning and creates another day.

SOME BOOKS TO READ

Hundreds of books collect or retell the myths of the world. This selection is no more than a starting-point; expeditions to the mythology or folklore sections of the library should lead to fascinating, unexpected finds.

General

Barber, R 1979 *A companion to world mythology*. Kestrel   Well-written, entertaining, useful.

Ions, V *The world's mythology in colour*. Hamlyn   Hundreds of spectacular photographs of the temples, landscapes and works of art associated with each myth. (For more Hamlyn books on myths, see Ions books mentioned below.)

Graves, R 1969 *The new Larousse encyclopaedia of mythology*. Hamlyn   Fat reference book, absorbing to browse in and invaluable for checking facts.

Others

Bailey, J ed 1981 *Men and gods*. Oxford University Press   Retold creation-myths and hero-legends from the world's religions. One of OUP's *Oxford Myths and Legends* series, which also contains short, lively books of *African Myths and Legends*, *German Hero-Sagas and Folk-Tales*, *Japanese Tales and Legends* and *West Indian Folk-Tales*.

Grimble, A 1952 *A pattern of islands*. Murray   A blend of folk-tales and personal memoirs by an ex-governor of the Pacific Gilbert and Ellis Islands. Light-hearted, witty and gentle; a perfect desert-island book.

Heyerdahl, T 1957 *Aku Aku*. Allen and Unwin   An account of Heyerdahl's exploration of Easter Island and his discoveries about its giant stone heads and underground magic caves. May not be mythology, but has the same throat-catching, mind-teasing power.

Ions, V 1983 *Egyptian mythology* and *Indian mythology*. Hamlyn   Detailed and well illustrated. As fascinating as her *World's mythology* mentioned above. Other recommended titles are *Japanese mythology* by Juliet Piggott, *North American Indian mythology* by Cottie Burland, *South American mythology* by Harold Osborne, *Oceanic mythology* by Roslyn Poignant and *African mythology* by Geoffrey Passinder. (All in the World's myths and legends series.)

McLeish, K 1983 *Children of the gods*. Longman   A complete retelling of the myths and legends of ancient Greece, with striking pictures by Elisabeth Frink.

48

NOTES TO ILLUSTRATIONS

The Twins (Japan) page 6: The figures in the painting are wearing kimonos as seen in a Japanese nineteenth-century silk painting of Isanagi and Isanami stirring the waters to create the first Japanese island called Onokoro.

Brahma and Sarasvati (India: Hindu) page 9: The painting shows the characteristics of Brahma and Sarasvati as seen in twentieth-century representations of this Hindu god and goddess. They both hold sacred texts and meditation beads. The instrument held by Sarasvati is a veena and Brahma also holds a lotus flower and a golden alms bowl.

The Dance of Life (Mexico) page 12: The Toltecs provide the roots of a myth-system which spread throughout the Central Plateau of Mexico. The Toltec God, Quetzalcóatl, the God of the Wind, was also the name of their semi-legendary priest and ruler. He appears in many texts and works of art. His headdress in the painting is based on one in a fresco at Bonampak, where a priest is arrayed as the plumed serpent, Quetzalcóatl.

How Light Became (New Zealand: The Maoris) page 21: The painting shows the various costumes of the Maòris; the traditional tattooed patterns of their faces are shown on Earth and Sky.

Seven Days (Middle East: The Bible) page 24: God is painted as a figure in the picture for Seven Days; although the artist is not bound by the religious laws of the faiths presented, she acknowledges that for Jews, Muslims and some Christian sects, who refer to this story, God is not represented in this way.

Giants and Gods (Northern Europe: The Vikings) page 27: The painting of the cow in this picture is the artist's impression of a Viking cow. No one is sure what they looked like, and the artist gratefully acknowledges the advice of A K Hufthammer, Zoological Museum, Bergen, Norway.

Old-spider and her Helpers (Island of Nauru) page 39: The spider in the painting is an Orb Web Spider from the islands in the Pacific Ocean. The artist gratefully acknowledges the help of Paul Hillyard, Natural History Museum, London, in identifying and providing a specimen to draw from.

The Five Sisters (Canada: The Thompson Indians) page 42: In the painting the costumes are based on those of Canadian Indians as seen in The Museum of The North American Indian, New York.

Ra (Egypt) page 45: The painting here follows that on a coffin from Butehamon in showing Nut, the Sky goddess, arched above Shu, the God of Air, and Geb, the God of Earth.